Bitcoin for everyone

Step by step guide for beginners

Learn the secrets to master

Bitcoin - Crypto - Trading Mindset

Staking - Stablecoins - Secure Wallet

Winning Strategies - Tips & Tricks

Francis Flobert

Evolutpress

To my son Leo

Curious, stubborn, determined.
Always one step ahead
of his young age.

- CONTENTS -

"Any fool can know. The point is to understand"
Albert Einstein

Promise

I start by making you a promise.

At the end of this book, I will reveal my secret to being profitable in the long run by operating in the cryptocurrency markets.

I discovered it thanks to John J. Murphy, the great author of the trading bible "Technical Analysis of Financial Markets" and thanks to the years I have dedicated to experimenting his techniques on my skin and on my money.

You will only be able to understand its greatness only if you have first read the other pages in the sequence in which I propose them. Each chapter is preparatory to the other, jump here and it would diminish the strength and great power that is in the book.

I only ask you to make this journey together until the very end. After that, fell free to express all the comments you want, I will accept them with open heart and hands.

In the book I did my best to avoid technical language and to make the contents easy and understandable to everyone, even those who do not know the topics at all.

Introduction

Bitcoin has grown by roughly **8,000%** (eight thousand percent) since it was first traded in October 2009. For just one dollar, you got **1309** (one thousand three hundred nine) bitcoin.

Today, at the time of publication of this book, it would be worth approximately **US $ 52 million**.

Crazy! True?

The question arises: can you become rich with trading?

Yes, it's true!

Can you lose all the invested capital with trading?

Yes, it's true!

But there is a whole world in between.

A world of opportunity and failure, of satisfaction and repentance, of right choices and regrets, of joy and fear, of anxiety and freedom, just like life.

Here's the bad news: **trading is not for everyone**.

It's an unfortunate statement, I know, but if I told you that anyone can trade and earn from it, I wouldn't be telling the truth. I notice this especially when I talk to people who are looking for a tip to get rich quickly. Or when they tell me they are tech-resistant and don't even want to learn how to send an attachment with an e-mail message.

Trading requires **training** diluted over time, to be blended with the **experience** gained in the field. But above all it requires an adequate mental attitude.

Here's the good news: these are all things that can be acquired with commitment and willingness to learn.

That's the purpose of this book: to make understandable all the topics in it, to make sure you can freely choose whether or not to enter this chaotic and fantastic world of the cryptocurrency market.

If you are good, as a result, you will be profitable over time.

...

You've surely heard of Bitcoin and the huge profits someone made in a very short time. People who in the space of a few years became multimillionaires starting at zero and companies born in a garage and who now manage billions of dollars.

Maybe a friend told you about it, maybe a work colleague made you attend a trade in which he earned a hundred dollars, maybe the world of finance and trading have always fascinated you but you never had the opportunity to see and understand how does it work.

Surely, reader, you could add your own "maybe" and the list would keep growing, but I'm here to answer your questions, even those that you haven't asked yourself yet, about the fantastic and inimitable world of trading.

A world of rules: some written, some unwritten.

The first rule you need to know is this:

Rule No. 1: "All that glitters is not gold."

...

Rights and legal notes

Chapter 1
Understanding Bitcoin and Blockchain once and for all

Who can answer the question: "what is Bitcoin?".
Take a minute and give it a try.

… … … … … …

… … … … … …

So?

Probably everyone will refer to something that has struck them most: from sensational news on television, to newspaper headlines, to comments at the bar and while you are in line to shop, to invasive social media ads that promise to make you rich with a click on the computer, lying in front of the sea while sipping a Mojito …

We hear around that Bitcoin is:

- a virtual currency
- a payment system
- a way to send and receive money
- a computer software
- the money with which to buy drugs
- a quoted currency that can be traded on an exchange like equities
- a reserve of money
- digital gold
- a system for making profit
- a system for losing money
- an IT platform
- a decentralized system
- a revolution for the financial system

- the currency of the future
- etc., etc.

Yes, it's true, it's partly true.

...

For me, explaining what Bitcoin is today is like when I tried to explain the Internet in the 90s.

One day I showed up for an appointment with the data processing center manager of a large international hotel chain to present an advanced and revolutionary hotel room booking system. My system allowed the potential customer of the hotel to see the hotel on his computer, to choose the room and to make a reservation.

All by himself.

What's strange, you say?

Oh yes, for today it is normal, but back then nobody had it.

Their Data Centre did not have an Internet connection, so I took a portable modem at 28kbp / s out of my bag and plugged in my computer that I had brought from home. The connection was unstable because the hotel's telephone network was very old and failed several times. Despite everything, I managed to complete my online presentation with some success, simulating on my online virtual hotel, built for the purpose, all the path that a customer would have to take to choose his room. Having accomplished my mission, I turned to the manager who, thick glasses and grey hair, had never stopped staring at my computer screen from behind his lenses. He was silent for a while then he looked me in the eye and said:

"In my opinion this Internet thing will never catch on"
"Why?" I asked.

"Ordinary people don't understand this and never will. As a computer scientist, I can understand the genius of your idea and do all the steps you did with your computer, but ordinary people..." he said, shaking his head with denial.

"Besides, how many people have computers at home, connected to the internet too?" he added annoyed.

"You are young, I advise you to devote yourself to more serious things than this internet. For example, in a subsidiary company, we are looking for a computer scientist graduated with honors to take care of the database, it is a stable and secure desk job, if you want I can arrange for you to have an information meeting" he added in a paternal tone.

I unplugged my modem, put it back in my bag, politely thanked him and said: "You have had your chance in life, I am looking for mine and I have immense confidence that one day the Internet will evolve and change this world to as we know it today ".

I shook his hand and left.

Do you see?

Everyone only sees what they want to see.

Bitcoin, in my opinion, is like the Internet in 1990.

Bitcoin is not just the whole of the list written above, but it is much more and now I will tell you why.

1.1 The genesis

Bitcoin makes its first whimpers on Halloween 2008 when a guy named Satoshi Nakamoto, who later turned out to be an invented name, posts a message to an encryption mailing list. The text said that he had been working on a new completely "peer-to-peer" electronic currency system that could operate without any other "third party *" (* i.e. credit card circuits, banks, PayPal, etc.). There was a link, still active, where you can download a pdf:

http://www.bitcoin.org/bitcoin.pdf

In nine pages of a document, Satoshi claimed to have found the solution for a new secure payment for the internet.

The pdf describes a new protocol which, using a peer-to-peer network, a proof-of-work protocol and public key cryptography, had solved all the problems that others like him, before him, did not have been able to find a solution, in an attempt to create the currency of the internet. An open system that allows those who are able to actively participate by implementing it, which **does not** need protection from hackers thanks to the decentralized and shared accounting ledger distribution system.

For many years scientists and computer scientists have been experimenting to create a digital currency, but without success. Satoshi, on the other hand, managed to combine the elements in a way that no one had ever thought of.

It was alchemy that invented Bitcoin.

Dense email exchanges followed with programmers and cryptographers who recognized his genius. The magnitude of his project was unmatched and they began to collaborate with him.

1.2 The blockchain

Satoshi seemed to come from the future and had foreseen everything.

But he was wrong. Not even he sensed that the **"blockchain"**, the ledger he invented, which validated the blocks in which the transaction is recorded, unchangeable and indelible, necessary to take into account the movements of bitcoins, is **what will change the world**.

Yes, because with the concept used to validate bitcoin transactions it will be possible to certify and validate everything: real estate cadastre, public administration, data archiving, automobile register, logistics, electoral votes, music rights, news certificates, educational qualifications, objects of art and jewellery, bottles of wine of controlled origin, agri-food products, cybersecurity, insurance and banking sectors, etc., etc., etc.

The Blockchain is **the explosive idea** contained in the brilliant idea of Bitcoin.

The **surprise** inside the Easter egg.

The fruit of sin.

If Bitcoin changes the way money is transferred and all global finance, the Blockchain will globally change the world as we know it.

Not even Satoshi, focused as he was on solving the problem of creating the internet currency, was aware of what and how many developments and repercussions would be over time with his blockchain.

Bitcoin and Blockchain are such revolutionary projects

that they bring with them the ability to subvert the pillars on which the undisputed rules of finance and the powers of the world economy have been based for centuries.

Rule No. 2: "The blockchain will revolutionize the world"

Things are already changing, in a few years nothing will be as we know it, just as it was with the advent of the Internet.

...

Eleven months after the first cry, in October 2009, the first exchange rate that fixed the value of bitcoin was published: by changing 1 dollar, 1309 bitcoins were obtained.

In 2010 the first bitcoin transaction for tangible assets was carried out: ten thousand bitcoins were paid for a pizza.

Towards the end of the year the price reached 50 cents of a dollar for 1 bitcoin and a sparkling ferment for the currency began to breathe in the air.

In that year the **Wikileaks** scandal broke out in the US. Due to his work, all donations towards Assange were blocked: Mastercard, Visa, PayPal, Western Union, they all had to refuse to accept them. At the same time, an article on PC World suggested using bitcoin as a solution to get around the obstacle and get donation funds to Wikileaks.

Satoshi replied on the forum to this article by writing the

textual words: **"It would have been nice to have this attention in another context. Wikileaks has knocked over a hornets' nest and the swarm is headed towards us"**.

This message was sent on December 11th, 2010, after which Satoshi disappeared from the forum and no one ever heard from him again.

No one had ever met him in person, no one knew his real identity. What remains of him is that 9-page document in which he explains his idea point by point. Bitcoin: an open source project gifted to the world. The unconscious spark of a financial big bang.

1.3 What is Bitcoin

Now I can finally tell you what Bitcoin is for me.

For me, Bitcoin is a **lifestyle**.

"Bitcoin" with a capital B, is the system, the infrastructure on which the "bitcoin" currency, with a lowercase b, rests, which is the virtual currency par excellence, the first digitally created, which can be bought, sold, traded on Internet. Usually these operations are carried out on computer platforms, called exchanges, which are platforms very similar to those of the stock market, from which bitcoin is separate.

There are many ways to **profit** from bitcoins and other cryptocurrencies born in the following years, the main one is trading: you buy bitcoins when the value is low and you resell it when it is high.

Sounds too easy, right?

The problem is that the price is very volatile and sometimes unpredictable.

You need to know how to move to avoid losing your capital.

In order to understand how to profit from bitcoins it is necessary to take a short and curious journey through time.

1.3.1 A curious journey through time

In the beginning was the barter.

The early man was a farmer, hunter or cattleman. The surplus of its production was used for the exchange of basic necessities.

There was no set price, the value of things was given by how badly they needed something. That is, the value that was attributed at that given moment to the object of exchange determined the price that one was willing to pay to get what was needed.

With the spread of trade and goods, they realised that it was not always possible to divide the exchanged goods, usually livestock, plus the weights and volumes of the goods certainly did not make life easy for those who had to move them by hand or on the back of a mule.

It became necessary to invent a system that was commonly accepted and whose value was recognized by the majority of people: the first forms of money were skins, cocoa, salt, shells ...

With the invention of metallurgy, the "strong powers" of the time invented a new system: **money**. Skins, cocoa, salt and shells were goods in the public domain, available in nature in large quantities, everyone could obtain them, but **minting coins** became the prerogative of the rulers.

With the creation of money came the banks.

Traces of the first banks can be found in the chronicles of ancient Greece, the first bankers, then called "trapezites" dealt with deposits and currency exchange. They were educated people, who could read and write unlike the rest of the population who were illiterate. Their main function was to act as guarantor. In those days, debts disputes were pretty common. But it sometimes happened that the creditor, despite the debtor having paid him, was smart and denied having received the money. It was the reputation of the two contenders that decreed the victory of the dispute, obviously at the expense of the truth.

To prevent this possibility, the debtor could go to the banker who, writing an official document, impartially certified that the sum due by the debtor had been deposited in his hands.

By its very nature, however, the banker, acting as an "usurer" started to lend the money stored in his lockbox, with interests.

This is how banks are born, precisely because of illiteracy.

The rise of banks in various cultures was unstoppable. Even kings and rulers needed bankers to finance themselves when the people's taxes were not enough and especially when they needed to finance their wars.

Including the last two world wars.

Banks lend money to the powerful to destroy.

Banks lend losers the money to rebuild.

Banks lend money to families to buy houses.

Whatever happens, the banks always win.

It is not my opinion, these are just facts.

At the end of the Second World War, the Western countries defined the rules to boost international trade at Bretton Wood. From 1944 the dollar was taken as a reference currency to which all other currencies were linked, with a fixed exchange value. To ensure the trust in the US dollar, it was **pegged to gold**, at a fixed price of $ 35 an ounce.

In practice it meant that it would be possible to bring dollars to the central bank and receive the corresponding gold in exchange.

The dollar was used as a reserve currency by all states, effectively allowing the US Treasury to print as much currency as they deemed necessary to relocate it to the world. Thus giving the dollar and the US enormous power.

In the 1960s, however, the situation began to arouse suspicion due to the exaggerated amounts of dollars circulating around the globe. French President De Gaulle asked for the conversion into gold of the dollar reserves held by the Bank of France and in his wake other states, which had doubts about the actual ability of the US Treasury to cope with the conversion, requested it.

In the end, it was the conflict in Vietnam that blew the bubble. The American Treasury was pouring rivers of money on the planet to meet the purchases made in the world to support the expenses of the immense needs of the American army in the conflict.

It was the point of no return. On August 15th, 1971,

President Nixon issued the proclamation that the dollar was no longer convertible into gold.

De facto uncoupling the dollar from gold created an earthquake in the foreign exchange markets, dark years of economic stagnation and high inflation began. With inflation came an indiscriminate increase in prices which, prolonged over time, led to a sharp decrease in the purchasing power of the currency.

The dollar thus lost its hegemony and its characteristic as a safe-haven asset.

In fact, how can something that the state mint can **reproduce and multiply indefinitely** be defined as a **"store of value"**?

It cannot, it's simple.

On the other hand, gold is a store of value because it is rare, not replicable and is subordinated to the concept of scarcity.

Bitcoin has the same characteristics as **gold** and even something more:

- It is increasingly **rare** due to the increasing mathematical difficulty of its computational extraction process.
- It is **not replicable**.
- It is **predictably scarce**.

While there could be the possibility that huge deposits of gold could come to light, causing its price to drop, for Bitcoin there is absolute mathematical certainty that, at the end of the extraction process, which could take place around the year 2140, there only **21 million** bitcoins could be in circulation. The strict mathematical rules of its protocols establish this: 21 million and that's it. At the time of writing, just under 19 million have been mined.

In his fascinating genius, Satoshi designed the bitcoin coin to be divided up to one hundred millionth, in practice eight decimals after the comma: 1.00000000 where the last decimal corresponds to 1 satoshi. This means that even fractions of bitcoins can be handled, any sum can be transmitted via a peer-to-peer network. This network is not administered by anyone, such as "uTorrent" used for the network exchange of files shared between users. In practice, there is no government or company that controls the traffic and value of bitcoins.

Chapter 2
Comparison between the traditional financial system and Bitcoin

- With the current traditional financial system, you are not the absolute owner of the funds on your bank account.
  With the Bitcoin ecosystem you have the **absolute monetary sovereign**ty of the funds.
- With the current traditional financial system it **only states** have the power to print money.
  With the Bitcoin ecosystem there is no such exclusivity.
- With the current traditional financial system, the economy is subject to **inflation**.
  With the Bitcoin ecosystem, this possibility does not exist because there can only be a **fixed number** of bitcoins.
- With the current traditional financial system you can be **excluded** or **marginalized**.
  With the Bitcoin ecosystem there is no such possibility, there is **no censorship**.
- The traditional financial system is **centralized**, all power and money reserves are in the hands of a few powerful and they can make all the decisions they want.
  The Bitcoin ecosystem is **decentralized**, no one owns it, no one controls it, everyone can participate and the internet on which it rests cannot be turned off.
- The traditional financial system is a **closed system**.

- The Bitcoin ecosystem is an **open system**.

2.1 Conclusions in comparison

- When the company you work for pays your salary to the bank, you are not the owner, but it is the bank that gives you credit when you need it. You then become the holder of a credit and not the absolute owner of your funds.
- With Bitcoin you have the absolute monetary sovereignty of the funds. Once deposited on the hardware wallet, you hold the keys, public and private, and no one can seize, foreclose or take them away at their unquestionable judgment. A regime of absolute freedom.
- The traditional financial system is based on exclusivity, only central banks can mint currency. Once it was linked to gold: so much gold a nation had, so much currency it could mint. But with a twist, a few years ago things changed. Global currencies are no longer linked to the underlying gold held in state coffers. Rulers may decide to print huge quantities of money and have demonstrated this in practice with the coronavirus pandemic.
- There will never be more than 21 million bitcoins in circulation
- People deemed unsafe in the credit environment, for example "bad payers", people subject to bankruptcy, etc., are prevented from accessing credit and in some cases the current system

provides for the **foreclosure** of funds held on bank accounts account holder at the request of the state or creditors.

- Bitcoins are **not fore closable** because there is no central authority that can intervene to do so. It is not an option allowed by the system.

- The traditional financial system is **centralized**, and there's a phenomena called "**single point of failure**": if the central servers, for example, shut down, or are cyber attacked, the bank will no longer be able to make ends meet, not they will know more how much money you had in your account, how many mortgage payments you have left to pay, and so on.

  The security protocols will sooner or later be able to reactivate the system, but in the meantime, for hours, days or weeks you will no longer have the money you had in your bank account. If the bank fails, anything can happen, including the risk of losing the funds of all account holders. **Cyprus** and Greece teach this to us, just to give an example not too distant in time. You can beat your fists on the ATM cash machine screen as much as you like, but if the bank cracked you can say goodbye to your money.

- Bitcoin and its blockchain are part of a **decentralized system**, a redistributed ledger on which transactions are indelibly recorded and certified. By its nature, being redistributed, it cannot be damaged by any hacker attacks.

- The traditional banking system is a completely **closed** system that does not allow sharing and interactions of external applications of other subjects other than the bank itself. Profit for the bank always comes first, innovation and the best customer service come much later.
- Bitcoin and its blockchain are an open system, on which software, platforms, services and applications can be implemented. The most advantageous for the whole system will be used and will thrive, creating wealth and greater freedom for all users, the others with little or no use will disappear thanks to the meritocratic system of natural selection.

Chapter 3
Creating the winning Mindset

I am a computer scientist and a chess player.

I started as a kid building my own computers, assembling all the used components that I could find anywhere, even in landfills. I still remember my first internet connection with an acoustic modem, found on the counters of a junk shop, the one where the handset of the old home telephone is inserted into a base with two cavities that houses it. The analog sound signal, through the sounds exchanged between microphone and receiver, is converted into electrical impulses allowing connection and dialogue with other computers.

It is called "acoustic coupler". Maybe you can find a copy at the museum.

It took a quarter of an hour to connect, twenty minutes to send a letter of a few lines to the receiving computer. Except that the connection dropped and it was time to start all over again. For me it was the most beautiful game in the world because, as a young explorer, I had made a conquest.

As an operating system, not being able to afford the one with windows, I used Dos which was free, but which had a textual and non-graphical interface like the current ones. The mouse was not included, so to do anything on the computer it was necessary to know by heart and type on the command line the right code with all the various parameters. If you got it wrong, that damn message would appear on the black computer screen: "error". Which gave no escape and which offered no solutions.

Over the years the rest came by itself, my insatiable passion has become my satisfying profession.

Chess, on the other hand, entered my life even earlier. I was seven and they arrived at Christmas with a distant relative in a package wrapped with wrapping paper. Despite my large family no one knew how to play, but a friend of mine at the time played with his father and he taught me the first strict rules that govern the game of chess.

At that time, I was too young to be attracted to girls, so after school we organized hours and hours of chess games and tournaments, meeting in turns in the houses of the players of the group that was gradually expanding. I read and learned everything that was then available at the municipal library of which I was the youngest member.

And it is still a passion that captivates me and has never abandoned me.

Years and years of games and studying attack and defence strategies have unwittingly forged me to understand and tame this fascinating world of cryptocurrency trading, a young world full of opportunities, tirelessly evolving, always on the move, always awake. Yes, because it is a world that never sleeps, 24 hours a day, seven days a week, including holidays.

When Western markets go to bed, Asian markets wake up and vice versa.

It's like being in a nightclub that has dozens of dance floors. You can stand on the edge and watch, you can dance with your favourite cryptocurrencies, you can stop and go out whenever you want but you know that anyway, others will continue to dance and maybe make money without you.

The techniques can be learned, but you have to build your own mental form and that is the structure that supports you. If passion drives you and captivates you then you are doubly blessed with luck, because instead of struggling, you will have fun and the joy that will ensue will be the fuel for your satisfaction and your profits.

...

How to create the winning mindset

Before moving on to operations and profits, it is essential to be sure that you have the **right mental attitude**.

We have seen in the previous pages the reasons and dynamics of the birth of money and Bitcoin and the characteristics of the current financial system.

Thanks to the comparison we have made, we should have clearer ideas of the context we are talking about. All of this was done in function of one of our main purposes: to create the **right mindset** to **profit from Bitcoin**.

To be successful in this field, you need a mindset that frees the mind from any preconceptions, that clears away false myths, that frees the eye from the traps present everywhere when it comes to money and finance and that does not make us prey to illusions.

Operating without the concepts learned with training

only does damage.

Do not believe brokers who promise that you will get rich in a short time, it's just a myth, they want to take you to their platform to earn with your money. Or to those who say that it is enough to copy the strategies of professionals to get rich. They forget that in trading, aside from techniques, one of the main aspects of tremendous importance is the psychological aspect of the trader. It is not by wearing someone else's suit that you become smarter.

Another example of something you should never ever do is to follow the **signals** of a chat on a **social** group. In most cases they are scams, they team together to get the unwary on a coin when the "**pump**" is running out, then they take the profits and the others are left with a fistful of flies in hand. Stay away.

Usually the common trader's approach is to focus on the **profit** of the operation. A right mindset, on the other hand, does the opposite: when you open a position, you focus on **risk management** and **capital protection**. The gain thus becomes the natural **consequence** of this attitude and not the main thing.

Technical analysis and graphs are not magical spheres: they do not reveal the future. They are just tools that tell us what happened in the past, allowing it to be represented graphically to give an idea of market trends, supports and resistances, in order to identify the risk that is encountered by opening a position.

With the right mindset the question we need to ask ourselves is not:

"How can I earn more?".

But: "How can I best minimize the risk of losses?".
There are three types of **risks** to watch out for:

- the **position** risk
  It is the one relating to the open position where we have already defined the percentage or sum of capital beyond which we are not willing to lose further.
- the **capital** risk
  It is that relating to a set of positions open on several fronts and beyond which we are not willing to lose further.
- the risk of **bankruptcy**
  It is the long-term risk of seeing capital drain out without making the necessary strategic changes.
  The end of the games!

...

There is no universal strategy, there are those who are **anxious** and are not comfortable with a **daily** time frame but relax with a weekly one. While there are those who feed on adrenaline and enjoy seeing the graph on an **hourly** time frame.

It is up to each of us to understand which are the positions that we can best manage and to frame the operations that match our own character.

Act accordingly to your feelings, especially at the beginning, then over time, with the necessary practice and training, you can get high, very high.

3.1 Goals

It is essential for the human mind to have goals to aim for in order to be successful.

I can't say what yours should be but I can tell you what mine are: "**wealth and freedo**m".

Being rich for me means living in abundance.

The luxury, the pomp, the ostentation of wealth disgusts me. In the long run they become a form of slavery, you are always competing with others and in the end you always come out with broken bones.

Wealth for me is having an abundance of time, opportunities, passions, love and money. Sure, money is not happiness, but it certainly helps to get it.

Freedom for me is the possibility of being able to choose always and in any case, without having to depend on anything or anyone.

Wealth and freedom are close relatives and, if they get along, they become soul mates.

Investing and trading allows you to have an **extra income**, a diversified income that with strategic planning makes money work for us and brings us closer to the goals that can radically change our lives.

Keeping the money in the bank account unused has now become just a cost, the cancer of inflation does the rest.

There are many ways to make profit: bonds, stocks, commodities, investment funds, cryptocurrencies, etc. Each with its operations, each with its degree of risk, each with its return on investment.

Personally, I chose Bitcoin and cryptocurrencies because according to my personal experience, if you know how to do it, there is currently no higher return on legitimate investments than this in the world. But you must be careful, **the risk is high**. This is why training is essential.

It is up to each of us to find the balance that can make

us rich, free and happy.

To get started with bitcoin it is not necessary to know everything about charts, technical and fundamental analysis, "market action", "open interest", "price action", trends, timing, supports, resistances, of moving averages, etc., etc.

We start from a base, perhaps the most basic possible, with a basic portfolio. You buy, sell and once you have confidence, you can start looking at slightly more speculative assets, to evaluate whether or not to take on some more risk in the face of a potential greater profit.

There is a whole world that must be discovered one step at a time.

Trading is based on the **odds** of gaining or losing when you **close a position**, so a lot depends on ourselves and not just the markets.

It is a long journey, which can be very rewarding, but which requires time and commitment.

Trading is setting up a **strategy** that is **profitable in the long ru**n: if my capital curve grows over time, it means that my strategies are working. It is normal to suffer losses, the important thing is to be **profitable in the long run**. To do this it is necessary to shift the focus from the single operation and concentrate on the **strategy**.

Whoever does not diversify and concentrate all the capital in a single position by "**all in**" is not trading but a **bet**, and it is madness!

You might as well go to the casino, bet everything on red and cross your fingers. But be aware that if black or zero comes out, you lose everything!

It is necessary to **avoid improvisation** by leaving the

emotion outside the door, as well as learn to accept that suffering losses is part of the training: who has never fallen while learning to ride a bicycle?

All this is possible only with careful strategic planning.

Rule No. 3: "Creating the winning mindset"

Here is the **checklist** of the key points to create the **winning mindset**:

1. define your goals
2. know your limits
3. know your strengths
4. understand the concepts to focus on
5. define what you want to achieve
6. define the time horizon, the time frame on which you are confidently able to operate
7. be aware that here one cannot improvise
8. be aware that training is needed

Chapter 4
Buying and selling bitcoins and criptocurrency

Let's now enter operations.

To profit from bitcoins it is necessary as a first step to **buy** them.

But before buying them you need to be clear with yourself what is the **main reason** why you want to deal with the King of internet coins, because based on this you will follow **different paths**:

1. as an **investment** and **accumulation plan** to practice.
2. as a **speculation** to **profit**
3. as a **store of value**

There will be different operational choices based on one's motivation, training, availability of capital and available time.

1. The **investment** aims to place savings in a valuable asset, savings that would otherwise remain fruitless. Little time is required for the investor to devote to training, as the aim is to know only those few **tools** in circulation to make the capital that you want to **profit** from. Obviously, the income will be commensurate as a percentage of the invested capital.

   If you are **new to the sector**, what I recommend is to start operating gradually, with a monthly bitcoin **accumulation plan** that requires very **little capital** and in the meantime you can begin to get informed and study the basic topics in order to start doing. trading. **Low weekly operativity** is required.

2. **Speculation** is aimed at making a **profit**, buying low and reselling high, monetizing the difference between buying and selling over a time horizon that can range from a few minutes to a few months. To do **speculative trading**, even a few hundred dollars are enough to start, but you need to have **a lot of time available** to follow the markets and to **improve your knowledge.** There will be a lot to **study** and keep up to date.
   Daily operativity is required.

3. If you want to use bitcoin as a **store of value**, no time is required to devote to it, but **considerable capital** is required. It is sufficient to buy the bitcoins, transfer them to an off-the-web hardware wallet and put it in a safe deposit box. It's like burying a treasure and waiting over the years for it to be worth bringing to light, regardless of what may happen in the markets.
   Virtually **no operation** is required.

...

As I wrote at the beginning of this book, one of the main purposes of this work is to understand the cryptocurrency market in order to be able to freely choose whether to enter or not. Therefore, we will now deal in greater depth with the first point relating to

profit from investment, **accumulation plans** and **low operativity trading**. As for speculative trading, we will see here the bases for operating, but due to the high level of trading, being a very vast and advanced topic, other specific books of mine are being planned. To see if they have been published in the meantime, try searching with the author's name.

Chapter 5
Investment, accumulation and low operativity trading

Ok, let's try to put ourselves in the shoes of a person who has never made investments in his life and is unaware of everything. Or in those of those who already have a small portfolio with securities that the bank made them buy and want to expand it with bitcoin. Both have heard that bitcoin is performing extremely well and do not want to miss the opportunity but they have never traded, they do not know technical analysis, they both work and do not have much time available to devote, so they would like to keep a **simple and relaxed** approach.

One of the best things a **newbie** can do is to start with a **three-component accumulation plan**:

1. an active management of the **purchasing** strategy

2. active management of the position with **periodic revaluation**

3. an **exit** strategy

First you need to know **how much** you can invest.

This aspect is very delicate, here is my opinion on it: **"Investing in cryptocurrencies can give high profits but it is a high risk operation, there is the possibility of losing all or part of the invested capital. Never invest more than what could create difficulties for the investor's standard of living"**.

If you have no idea how much to invest, it is preferable to avoid choosing a random number: the simplest method to quantify it is to set a reference date every month, always the same. Let's say, for example, the last day of the month. Every month on that date you sit down at your desks and calculate how many resources you can devote to your active investment. A simple mathematical calculation is sufficient: the **total income** of the month minus the **total fixed expenses**, a **percentage** must be calculated on the result, say 10%, 20%, it's up to you, which can be **allocated to the investment** in a way that this subtracted amount won't cause any inconvenience in the normal economic management of the personal or family budget.

Example: $ 3,000 in net income - $ 1,500 in fixed expenses = $ 1,500, considering that you also have to live with this money: going out to dinner, to the cinema, flowers for the girlfriend or boyfriend...

You have to ask yourself: out of this amount, how many dollars can I dedicate that month investment without causing me problems?

If, for example, you subtract 15%, that is $ 225 to devote to the investment, can it be done? Obviously, everyone has to deal with his real situation.

So, we said, you keep 15%, that is 225 $ based on this example and you buy bitcoin. (How to buy we will see in the next chapter).

Every month you make this personal budget operation and quantify how much month by month you can afford to invest without this creating problems for your standard of living. On the basis of the monthly income and expenses that will never be the same, you will decide from time to time the amount to be dedicated for the purchase of bitcoins.

Thus, actively balancing your investment position with a monthly accumulation plan.

After at least one year of accumulation you can begin to make an initial balance and evaluate the possibility of taking a **part of the profit**. If the gain was excellent, you can think of withdrawing 5 or 10% of the accumulated capital.

The **timing** of any exit must be much longer, half-yearly or yearly, than the one used for entry, which is monthly.

There will have been months in which you bought more and others less, the capital in the meantime, also based on the performance of Bitcoin, lends itself to a check to evaluate whether to leave everything and continue, whether to take the excess that has grown compared to the capital paid, if the entire position of the savings plan is to be liquidated in a fractional manner.

You are probably wondering: "**when do I withdraw all my capital?**".

Unless there are sudden emergencies or extreme necessities, I am suggest you not to liquidate everything, I would keep a part in my portfolio anyway.

I personally am a convinced "**holder**". When I first bought bitcoin the market price was less than $ 3,000 and despite its fluctuations it is now worth $ 61,000 at the time of writing. So you will understand how I can be motivated not to sell since it has grown more than twenty times as much over the years.

In my opinion, over time, it will grow more, much more.

Institutional investors and large investment funds are starting to trade bitcoins, attracted by the stratospheric profits, unimaginable with other traditional financial assets, and this is acting as a driving force, creating ever greater confidence in other large and small investors.

I don't know what will happen in the future, there are no certainties, but as I have already told you, in my opinion bitcoin and the blockchain are a **philosophy**, which I carefully study in its developments every day.

Mine is not an act of blind faith, they are just evaluations with a cold mind, with knowledge of the facts: this is why I am optimistic about its growth.

Always remember, however, that Bitcoin and cryptocurrencies are a **high-risk asset**, which is why you need to have the right **mindset**.

There were months when my savings plan was at a big loss because the market had collapsed and the value of my capital had become half of the total money I had invested. Fear made it necessary to sell everything to at least try to avoid losing again. There have been days when prices have skyrocketed and the capital had quickly become double the money invested, the temptation to sell everything in those moments is very strong. But if you are not an experienced trader don't do it, it could be the first of a long series of mistakes you could make.

With the same emotionality with which you have sold everything, you could then be tempted to buy everything back as soon as the price goes down, but not knowing the technical analysis, you would hardly find the entry point of a downhill price, which loses ten or twenty thousand dollars in a few minutes. Fear would then make you resell at a price much lower than what you bought back at in an attempt to limit the damage.

Frustration and anguish will not allow you to sleep and you will probably spend the night glued to the screen checking the graphs and cursing the day when it occurred to you to invest in bitcoin. Quite the opposite of the initial premise of maintaining a "**simple and relaxed**" approach.

To win you need to have the right mindset and follow the initial strategy without being controlled by emotions.

Chapter 6
How to buy bitcoins

To buy bitcoins you need to sign in and use a platform called "**exchange**".

The cryptocurrency exchange is an IT platform on which you can **buy, sell and make other transactions** on cryptocurrencies, including **buying and selling bitcoins**.

In the traditional stock market there are operating hours, while the world of cryptocurrencies never closes. It is always in constant turmoil, 24 hours a day, seven days a week, on a planetary level. When the western markets go to bed, the Asian ones wake up and vice versa: a running train, practically unstoppable.

To participate and be operational, it is necessary to choose at least one exchange platform on which to practice. There are many, each with its own specific characteristics, but still very similar to each other from an operational and visual point of view. It is an important choice and should not be made by chance.

Among the many exchange platforms in the world, one must not fall into the error of thinking that one is worth the other. You must know how to read what is behind the screen and to do so, just inquire.

Remember that you are giving them your money.

Rule No. 4: "Find out about the company you entrust your money to"

...

In the context of this book, for practical exercises, I must choose at least one platform to show you how to operate. My choice falls on the "Kraken" exchange. I'll show you step by step how it works, after which you can be **up and running immediately**.

I specify that I have no interest that you choose Kraken or another exchange, the reasons only concern **rule n. 4**. If you already use another exchange platform or prefer to operate without Kraken, feel free to do so and keep in mind that all the steps described below describe characteristics and operations that are present more or less also in the other exchange platforms. Maybe they will be in different positions or they will not be called exactly the same but, in essence, the musicians change but the music is the same.

In my opinion Kraken, as of the day of this writing, is the Ferrari of exchanges, but the reason why I chose to talk about it is this: the exchange must be **regulated** and to be so it must undergo strict controls relating to security and current laws. Other important factors are that: the more known and famous it is, the more years it has been active and the higher the safety standards.

Last but not least, the platform must be easy to understand and use, must have the most recent services, excellent customer care and must be reliable. All of the above, in my opinion, are met by Kraken.

Be free to choose but remember that your safety and your capital must always come first.

Rule No. 5: "Prevention is better than cure".

Kraken is universally recognized as one of the safest exchanges in the world for the security standards it uses. It is one hundred percent **regulated** and even has a **banking license**, one of the few in the world that has managed to obtain it.

6.1 Operating on the exchange platform

On the exchange platform it's possible to buy and sell cryptocurrencies, with instant transfer and extremely advantageous fees, buy crypto using other cryptocurrencies and use the "futures" platform for those who want to implement speculative operations at the highest levels.

It also provides the "staking" service to obtain an interesting passive income on many coins.

Here we will discuss all the important points to become fully operational: from **opening the account** to **maximum security**, including operations

on **how you can buy and sell** and **transaction fees**.

Let's see them step by step.

I recommend that you open the official website of "kraken.com" on one of your devices so that you can follow me better.

1) Account registration and security

Registering an account takes just a few minutes, all you need is an email, password and one of the following: identity card, driving license or passport.

Once entered the data and registered, the platform system will carry out the identity verification process, an operation that can last from a few hours to a couple of days. They must have proof that it is really you.

Usually an email arrives informing you that the verification was successful, at which point we log into the account and **secure it**.

This is an imperative: "It is absolutely essential to **maximize the security of your account**".

Fortunately, Kraken has a very high level of security, step by step, which is very simple to implement.

Go to your profile menu and click "security", then settings, then **"two-factor authentication"**: enabling it will ensure that you are the only one able to access your account, even if someone else knows your password.

By enabling the "two-factor" every time a deposit or a withdrawal of funds is made, the system will require two-factor authentication.

Enabling is optional, but if you too are one of those who are thinking: "Well I'll start now, **I'll take care of protecting the account later on**", **you're wrong!** Some don't enable it, then cry when they lose all their money to a virus or a phishing email that steals their credentials.

You are protecting your assets, your investments, get out of mental lethargy and enable two-factor authentication.

The two or more-factor authentication is based on the same system that is used to enter your bank's online account: user and password. The bank then asks for another data, that is a numerical sequence generated by another technological channel: a token, the bank's app, a text message, etc.

With Kraken, as an additional channel, you can use the "authenticator" app of the largest search engine. For android phones, download the app and follow its instructions. With the devices of the bitten apple follow the instructions on the support websites, it is very simple.

If you use another exchange platform, the procedure is certainly similar to the one described above.

...

Done?

Secured your exchange platform account?

Okay, now that we've finally finished the most boring, but crucial part, we can start having fun.

2) Deposit of funds

To start having fun and possibly earning money, you need to **deposit funds**. So, enter your account profile, select the "**deposits**" menu, you should be redirected to a page with a list of all accepted fiat currencies: dollar, euro, pound, yuan, etc. Click on "**deposit**" next to the fiat currency you want to deposit and you will enter a page where you have to choose the deposit method: I recommend "clear junction" which allows you to make **instant transfers**, in order to get the funds to the exchange platform immediately to be able to use them right away, with negligible fees.

The data to be used to make the transfer to your online bank appears. As the **recipient** of your bank transfer, copy the **IBAN** of the exchange platform; in the **memo** of the transfer you have to **copy and paste** the alphanumeric string that you see appear under the reference including the writing "kraken.com", insert the whole string, making just copy and paste. Once the transfer has been made, the funds will be immediately credited to your account. I insist by advising to copy and paste because if you make transcription errors the funds will be sent back, or they could ask for the identification of an even higher level, with the verification of the residential address.

And it's just a waste of time.

For the **withdrawal** it is exactly the same thing, if you want to withdraw dollars or euros, select the chosen currency, select the "clear junction" method, also in this case there is an instant transfer, you will be shown the fees, also in this case very low.

3) Deposit cryptocurrencies

In addition to the deposit of fiat currency, it is possible to directly deposit bitcoins, coming from other exchanges or other wallets. The procedure is very similar to fiat currency deposits and withdrawals.

To **deposit bitcoin**s, click on deposit, the system will generate a new address. It will be sufficient to copy and paste that string into the sending interface of the person making the crypto deposit to receive the bitcoins.

Be careful, you can only have a maximum of five addresses active at the same time, if you create one more, the oldest one will expire after seven days, so be aware that you cannot generate an infinite amount of addresses. If you generate more than five, the older ones will expire. This does not mean that you lose the accredited bitcoins but only that in the future you can no longer use the expired address.

As for the withdrawal fees, they are low, much lower than the competition. To withdraw bitcoins, for example, there is a fee of 0.00015 bitcoins. Considered that other exchanges apply 0.0005 it's pretty clear that it is much cheaper, practically less than a third.

Again, you simply need to add an address to your "white list" and confirm it with two-factor authentication. The address remains saved, in order to have a white list of reliable addresses.

4) Deposit of currency by credit card

As an alternative to wire transfer, you can deposit funds using a **credit** or **debit card** but be aware that the fees are much more **unfavourable**.

So, in my opinion, it is preferable to make an instant transfer rather than using the card.

5) Buy bitcoin or other cryptocurrencies

Once the money is in your account on the exchange platform, you can buy bitcoins.

How do you make your first bitcoin purchase?

Let's see immediately the simplest method, which however has the highest fees.

It is designed for those who want a simple and large "**buy**" button and an unmistakable "**ok**".

You can always find it in your account under the heading "**buy crypto**".

Choose which currency you want to buy, for example bitcoin, how much you want to spend, for example in dollars, the "buy" button appears below, just one click and it's done.

Amazingly simple.

The **sale** and **conversion** from one crypto to another work with the same mechanism.

Ok, this is the **simplest way ever** to buy and sell or

convert bitcoin or crypto on the exchange.

On this screen you can also **add a credit or debit card** and make a direct purchase through it, but beware of **transaction fees**, because simplicity pays off!

To purchase by **credit card**, you pay a **fee of 3.75% plus a small fixed fee**, unlike the purchase with an instant bank transfer which has no fees to pay because a spread is applied on the market value of the coin purchased. Exchanges don't do charity.

Simplicity is very nice, but I **don't** recommend using these two purchasing methods. With a little patience and desire to learn, I will show you the way to save **many, many fees.**

6) Purchase of cryptocurrencies on the traditional platform

To benefit from a decent operativity and **low fees** we will place buy or sell orders directly on the platform, but **not** yet the one used by professional traders that we will see immediately after.

Here we are still on the simplified path.

In this case **fees drop a lot** and will still go down as the volume handled increases: between 0 and 50,000 dollars of purchase, fees are 0.26% on the "taker" or "market order", while 0, 16% on the "maker" or "limit order".

To use the traditional exchange there are two types of interfaces which can be accessed by clicking "**trade**" on the main menu.

At the top is the traditional interface, which has three difficulty levels: **simple, intermediate and advanced**.

Each level adds **optionals** to orders from time to time,

which can be customized more and more by adding the elements that we will now see.

a) simple interface

Let's start from the simple traditional one, which is actually the easiest of all, it is immediate and if one just wants to buy or sell, without trading, I think this is the most immediate method.

Step 1

Choose the market, that is the pair of coins on which you want to trade, for example bitcoin / dollar (on Kraken bitcoin is represented by the acronym **XBT** instead of the usual **BTC**, do not be scared, it simply has a different way of writing bitcoin. It's not a derivative, it's nothing strange, it's bitcoin).

Step 2

Here you can buy or sell bitcoins.

By selecting the "**market**" type order, you buy XBT at the current market price and pay the "**taker**" commissions at **0.26%**.

Example: I want to buy 0.0005 bitcoins, the system automatically calculates the value in dollars at the current market price, click on "**buy**", the order is **immediately executed** and that's it.

Another option is selecting "**limit**" choosing in this case to buy at a lower market price and pay "**maker**" fees at **0.16%**. In practice, if the price drops to the price I set, the purchase is triggered and with the same amount I will have more bitcoins than I would have if I had bought at the market price.

Example: Let's say that bitcoin is now trading at $

*60,000, according to my technical forecasts I believe the trend will be bearish, I assume it could reach the 55,000 range, so I'm going to place my "**limit**" order at $ 55,000. With one click I place it on the **order book** at that price.*

If bitcoin does not go down to that price, the order will never be executed, but if it goes down it will be executed and I will have bought at 55,000 instead of 60,000 dollars with commissions only 0.16%.

*In practice, if I had bought with the "**market**" type order I would have bought **immediately** at 60,000, instead with the "**limit**" type order, if my forecasts are correct, I am in **no hurry** and the price drops to the hypothetical figure of the example, that is 55,000, I made a considerable **saving** by giving myself a discount of 8.33%.*

...

Here is a very useful tool:
- <u>The formula for calculating the discount percentage</u>
It is very simple to use and I am sure it will be very useful, it is the formula used in the previous example:
Starting price - discounted price / starting price x 100 =% discount
60,000-55,000 / 60,000 x 100 = 8.333%

...

For the "**limit**" **sale** it's exactly the same thing but in reverse.

If I make a purchase by selecting **limit**, it is obvious that my price must be lower than the current market price, otherwise there is no saving.

If, on the contrary, I want to sell, the limit price must

obviously be higher than the current price, otherwise there is no profit.

b) intermediate interface

With this option some details are added.

- There is the option to postpone the market order, that is, I can enter it now, but I can also select the date when it becomes operational on the market, for example tomorrow at noon. There is also the option to expire, in case it was not successful, to cancel the order, for example at midnight. All without any additional commissions.
- It's possible to choose whether to pay commissions in bitcoins or dollars.
- There is the possibility to use "margin trading". This is **"spot"** margin trading, it is not about **"futures"** which we will see better later. With the spot margin trading the commissions are double: those at the opening, which are added to the classic commission, plus the commissions every 4 hours to keep the loan open.

  With margin trading in practice, you amplify your position by using much more capital than you own, capital **borrowed** from the exchange or from other traders. In exchange, a **fraction** of your capital at stake is asked for deposit. Operating in **leverage** enable to amplify one's position.

  The leverage defines the exposure and quantifies the amount that goes into escrow: 2x, 5x, 10x, even 100x. The greater the leverage the greater the amount required in deposit, if it is successful the gains are high but otherwise the losses are large.

For example: with 10x leverage to operate with a capital of 100,000 dollars you have to deposit 10,000.

In a low volatility market such as forex, the risk is more calculated, but for the crypto market which is very volatile, to use margin trading you must be truly expert and very often even experts come out with broken bones.

My advice is to take the step according to your own leg.

No margin trading for beginners.

c) advanced interface

For those who want to make a complete trade, the advanced option finally allows you to enter the heart of the orders, allowing you to enter other important parameters.

1. **Market**
2. **Limit**
3. **Stop loss**
4. **Take profit**
5. **Stop limit**
6. **Take profit limit**
7. **Save position**

Let's see them together:

- **Market** and **limit** are the two way to enter the market orders that we have already seen before.

- The **"stop loss"** is very important. It is an automatic setting that is used to minimize losses in our absence, by accurately establishing how much we are willing to lose on a position. It is a money management tool that allows us, once set up, to stay relaxed even if we are not controlling the markets.

  Let's make a practical example by following the options available in the advanced interface: I want to issue a buy order at the market, for 0.1 bitcoin, without leverage, I start from now until I cancel the order myself, paying the fees in dollars, with conditional "stop loss" closure.

  To protect my order I can fix a price in dollars, for example: bitcoin is traded at $ 60,000, I insert the stop loss at $ 50,000, so if it drops suddenly I cut the losses to 50,000 without going further. Or I can choose the option that if it is lowered for example by $ 1,000, I close the order at a loss only for that amount.

  Or as a percentage, for example if the price drops by 5% I close the order at a loss only for that percentage.

  The stop loss is the thing that allows us to go to bed and sleep peacefully. It is the watchdog of the position that remains open in our absence.

- **Take profit** is a tool that works in the same way as the stop loss, but instead of cutting the losses closes the order when we have reached the profit we had established.

For example: the market price of bitcoin is 60,000, I set the take profit at $ 70,000, so if it rises to that price, the take profit closes the order without my intervention and I make a profit of $ 10,000.

Stop loss and take profit are used to protect a position when we are busy doing something else and are recommended for those who trade and not for those who only make simple purchases.

- **Stop limit and take profit limit** I personally don't use them.

The difference is that, in addition to entering the stop price, you must also enter the limit price.

What does it mean? In the stop loss, if the price falls below a certain threshold, the stop sells, in the stop limit, if the price falls below the established threshold he goes to insert a limit order, obviously we must also enter the limit price at which to place the order.

Example: I enter a buy order, the stop price must be higher than the current price and it is an order that basically tells the exchange that if the price reaches a certain price it must issue a buy order at my price, which is the limit price. This was the example for the purchase order.

For the sale: if the price falls below a certain threshold, I enter a sell order at the price I previously set, which is the limit price.

As I said before, I personally hardly ever use them. While instead I prefer to use the classic stop loss and take profit.

In my opinion, the stop limit makes sense if set above a price resistance so that if the price pumps up there then it enters the order at the price of the resistance. That way it would make sense.

- **Save position**, it is used to add margin in case of leverage position, which for the moment I strongly advise against for beginners.

6) Pro platform and cryptocurrency purchase.

Another interface is the "**Pro**" one, finally the one for advanced traders, which can be accessed by clicking the small icon that represents a graph on the top menu. In my opinion, the Pro interface is much more immediate and intuitive than the traditional one.

Thus we enter the **temple** of trading.

Black screen bottom, central candlestick chart, order book, moving averages, RSI, Bollinger bands, Fibonacci ... Here is everything you need to trade and more: a complete platform.

The website was once called Crypto Watch, it was basically acquired by Kraken who built its pro platform on top of it.

- All the things we saw earlier can be applied on the "pro" without **moving elsewhere** and above all by keeping an eye on the price and volume **chart**.
- To operate you must choose the **pair of coins** on which you want to buy or sell, the choice of the pair of coins can be placed in the favourites by clicking on the star to always have it highlighted in the preferred currencies.

- You can choose the **time frame**, that is the time horizon in which you want to analyse the price changes: from a few minutes to years.
- You can insert some technical analysis indicators and oscillators.
- You can choose the types of candles to represent market trends, bar and line charts, etc.
- It is very customizable: you can go to insert drawings, lines and text boxes, in short, you can really configure it as you like.
- The depth chart is also visible, i.e. the visual graph of what is on offer and in demand on the order book of the currency we are observing.
- Then we have the order book itself and the list of executed trades.
- On the right instead we have the order panel which is very compact, very simple: either buy or sell and the type of order.
- Finally, below we have quantity, price and all those fields that we have seen a little while ago: market, limit, stop loss, etc., (of which I invite you to re-read their functioning in the previous pages), but all compacted in a single box.

I personally find the Pro platform much more comfortable. There is nothing more and nothing less than what we have seen before in the traditional platform. Only the layout and graphics change.

The leverage in this case is a slider that slides from 1x up to 5x.

Obviously, the commissions are exactly the same, only the graphical interface changes.

7) Futures

If the trading experts want to opt for a more speculative operation, as I said before it is advisable, compared to the use of the margin trading spot, to use "Kraken futures". There is leverage of up to 50x, with much lower fees and higher liquidity.

To access from the "deposits" page, click on "account balance", click on "futures trading". You are redirected to Kraken futures which has a very similar interface to the pro one. To login you can use the same account used on the trading platform, there's no need to create another one.

The first important point to **understand** is **how futures work and what the difference is**.

The futures you find on Kraken are the so-called **"inverse perpetual"**.

Inverse means that they use not the stable dollar USDT as collateral (see next chapter), but another coin, for example: bitcoin / dollar has bitcoin as collateral.

Perpetual means that they are derivatives with no maturity, therefore futures that do not expire, but have the so-called "funding" that keeps them linked to the price of the underlying.

How does it work? Every hour this *funding* rate is paid by *long* to *short* or vice versa, if the rate is positive it means that longs pay to short and if it is negative short pays to long. This is conceived to keep the price of the perpetual linked to the underlying.

Once you understand this, you have to deposit bitcoins if you want to trade on Bitcoin / dollar, Ethereum if you want to trade on Ethereum / dollar, etc.

But as I have already told you these are not things for beginners, those who want to operate with margin trading and futures must have acquired more than good experience in the field, because here mistakes are very expensive.

However, **there is a demo account on Kraken for those who want to practice**.

8) Staking

Staking is very interesting for those who want to **make income** from some of the cryptocurrencies that they do not use. In practice, coins are tied up to get a **reward**, it is very advantageous and you get paid for doing nothing at all.

Beautiful, Isn't it?

It is like when, years ago, the banks gave interests to keep money in the account, while now it is account holders who in fact have to pay the banks in order to keep the money.

Clicking on the top menu "staking", the page with the currencies that can be rented opens.

Staking is very simple, just enter the amount you want to bind in this staking account and confirm. The staking amount is deducted from the spot account and is entered in the staking account.

To untie them it is the same thing exactly in reverse.

It is extremely simple, zero commissions and is very convenient for those who want to make an income from the coins they do not use.

The annuity percentages are good and vary based on the

currency and staking plan chosen.

...

To conclude this presentation, I recommend that you practice a lot, at first **without completing the purchase and sale orders**, but keeping a written record on an excel sheet or on a diary. When you feel confident enough try placing a few orders of a few dollars to see if you understand how it works and if things are going as they should. After that, within a few days, things will start to flow and you will go faster. Remembering that the above rules and methods, once learned, are valid on most exchanges.

Rule No. 6: "When you learn to ride a bicycle, you know how to do it with all bikes".

There are many exchanges in the world but remember that your safety and your capital must always be first.

Prevention is better than cure.

Chapter 7
Stable coins

It would be nice and exciting to shop by paying in bitcoins.

If it weren't for the fact that since you left the house, parked the car, filled the trolley at the shelves, queued at the cash desk, the price of bitcoin has changed so many times that, perhaps, your beer costs double or maybe half of when you left the house.

This problem is due to the volatility of the asset.

There is a second important factor to take into consideration: what incentive do I have to pay for a coffee with bitcoins if I know that it is an asset that increases in value over time?

Bitcoin is a store of value.

Would you pay for coffee with gold?

This is one of the reasons why stable coins were invented.

The stable coin is a digital currency, just like other cryptocurrencies and as the name suggests it has a constant value. It does not devalue and does not increase in price: it remains constant.

In fact, in order to operate on exchanges, you need to exchange your fiat currency (dollar, pound, euro ...) with a stable coin. With this stable coin, therefore, you can buy cryptocurrencies.

It could be said that the stable coin is the currency that gives access to operate on the cryptocurrency markets.

It is not issued by any government agency, it is digitally created in a blockchain by the company that issues it.

Question: will it be safe?

The value of a coin cannot appear out of nowhere as if by magic, otherwise each of us could get up in the morning and sell the coin they dreamed of creating overnight. What value would it have and above all who would be willing to buy it?

Stable coins are linked to a valuable asset or another currency.

To guarantee a stable coin, the company that issues it should deposit a value corresponding to the coins it puts into circulation with a ratio of 1 to 1.

Example: one million stable coins = one million dollars pledged as collateral.

7.1 Examples of stable coins

There are many stable coins, each with its own characteristics: centralized or decentralized, some regulated, others not, some safe, others not.

Let's see together the most capitalized, therefore the most important.

We will evaluate them taking into account the usefulness and risks of each.

- **USDT Tether**

  It is the oldest and most used of them all, but also the most criticized.

  Tether saw the light in 2015, it currently has a capitalization of around $ 37 billion and is constantly growing.

  It is centralized and linked to the US dollar as an underlying collateral. In theory it should have a ratio of 1 to 1, i.e. each USDT issued should have a US dollar as its deposited value.

In reality, this has not always been the case. The elusive attitude of the company that issues Tether has never allowed the certainty of being able to verify how many dollars were held in guaranteed deposit on its accounts. The company reserves the right to make fractional reserves, just like banks do. That is, a liquid part remains on the escrow account and the other part, the larger one, is dedicated to loans and investments.

Until recently, it was known about Tether USDT that a quarter of the capitalization was deposited in escrow accounts.

A dispute is underway with the US federal authorities to certify its regulation and it seems they are finding a fair deal for everyone.

Despite all this, USDT is the most used and most capitalized stable coin on most exchanges.

Much of its success is also due to the fact that with Tether it's possible buy and sell most of the cryptocurrencies on the market, while with other stable coins the possibility of trading is much more limited.

- **TUSD TrueUSD**
  Born in 2018, market capitalization around 280 million dollars, it is centralized and is pegged to the US dollar. Unlike the previous one, it is regulated and the situation of the company issuing it is transparent. It is a younger stable coin

than Tether but which promises well because it has all the credentials.

- **PAX Paxos Standard**
  Born in 2018, market capitalization of around 800 million dollars, in addition to being centralized, it is regulated and approved and supported by the financial services department of the New York Stock Exchange.
  Which perhaps if on the one hand it earns it trust and reputation, on the other, in the relatively free world of cryptocurrencies, it does not take off for this very reason.

- **DAI Maker Dao**
  Year of birth 2017, market capitalization of about 91 million dollars, it is decentralized and born precisely to be against the tide, to be disconnected from traditional currencies and not subject to the financial authorities.
  DAI Maker Dao lives and thrives on the Ethereum blockchain and maintains stability thanks to its smart contract.
  As a positive aspect, decentralization has on its side, on the other hand, the fact of having software that governs it makes it more volatile than the others and potentially sensitive to cyber attacks

There are many more stable coins, each with its own peculiarities. But my job here is not to make the list and descriptions of all the stable coins in the world, you can easily go to the coin market cap website which lists all the cryptocurrencies, including the stable coins. It offers its main features, the current price and market capitalization.

My speech tends to make people understand what stable coins are, why they exist, what they are for and why they interest us.

I cannot tell you which one to use to operate on the markets. Personally, I can tell you that I usually use the first two: TUSD and USDT. The first for the guarantees it offers and the second, despite being much talked about, for the numerous couple possibilities it offers to trade and because it is accepted on most exchanges.

But to each his own choice.

Chapter 8
Traders' enemy No. 1: "Emotions"
- How to win FOMO and Panic Sell -

Emotionality: no one is immune to it.

We are human beings, emotionality is part of us, in an indissoluble way.

Emotion is important and it is the way in which we human beings react psychically and somatically to the environment around us. Emotionality is that thing that makes us react suddenly and abruptly to a situation. If the reactions are proportionate to the stimulus they can be defined as normal, which means that we act **in favour of ourselves.** But if the reactions are disproportionate, inadequate, excessive in intensity and duration then, beyond the concept of normality, the reactions put into practice could be **against ourselves**.

For example, a feeling of tenderness towards a puppy that looks at us from behind the bars of a kennel can lead us to make a donation to an association that takes care of animals without a family. The benefit for us will be a consequent state of psychophysical well-being for having done good and for being activated in this support campaign.

Take the opposite example.

Let's say we are driving a car, at an intersection we are not given the right of way, anger drives us to insult first and then to chase the unruly motorist who, out of fear or wisdom, does not want to stop. The anger rises during the entire time of the chase in which we play wildly until the other stops and then, once we get off, we punch him until he goes to the ground unconscious.

It is an extreme example, I know, but it has all the characteristics necessary to show that it is excessive, inadequate, excessive, lasting, intense.

In trading there is no need to be so extreme. Let's take the example of a novice trader who, after trusting the **rumours** circulating on **social media**, enters with a purchase of $ 1,000 on bitcoin, but has chosen the **wrong time** to enter, it's too late, now the pump is running out. The selloff of all those who bought low and reached the profit point they had established at the entrance (take profit) begins.

When there is a mass sale, especially close to a key or psychological figure, I know 30,000 or 40,000 for example, looking at the chart with a narrow time frame, it seems that the market collapses as if there is no tomorrow.

When you are losing money, which perhaps you could not afford to lose, in contravention of one of the fundamental rules of the successful trader, emotionality can play tricks.

Our victim suddenly realizes that he has forgotten to put a stop loss to protect him.

Panic!

The fear of losing money immobilizes him because he doesn't know what to do. Then he goes to the social chats, the same ones from which he got the bad information for the purchase entry point, and meets only desperate people, who like him are looking for a foothold so as not to drown in their own emotions. The first one who writes: "I sell everything" receives the same effect as a room full of people in a cinema in which someone shouts: "Fire!".

It is the "save yourselves!".

In the general confusion our terrified trader follows the fleeing herd and sells at the bargain price of the moment to try to stem the huge losses.

A catastrophe!

I assure you that these dynamics occur every day, but only to those who do not protect themselves with the right mindset and an adequate risk management strategy.

Rule No. 7: "Never be controlled by emotion"

...

8.1 Emotions are very important

In emotions, what makes the real difference is between **experiencing** them and **be a victim** of emotions.

Living the emotions allows you to be **free** to feel affection, to love, to rejoice, to be the captain of your own ship.

Being **subjected** to emotions **enslaves** us, doing things that in a state of lucidity would never have been done. Justifying ourselves after doing something nonsensical with a "he was stronger than me".

Alternatively, some use only **logic** as a North Star, falling, in my opinion, into the opposite trap, that of becoming a computer without any emotion. Prey to the coldness that dries up the heart, without poetry in life.

So, what is the solution?

There is a phrase that I love, it is from an Indian sage who says this:

"Do not insist on looking for the solution, if you find the balance, it will be the solution".

Even a successful trader can miss an entry point and forget a stop loss.

- But if he has invested, he will have made his fundamental analysis carefully and with full knowledge of the facts.

- If he has invested it is because he believes in it, not because they have only suggested him on social media.

- If he sees the market collapse, he first of all keeps calm, remains lucid, picks up his technical analysis charts on which he has clearly marked the supports and resistances of the coin, analyses the trend and tries to re-read the signals. With a good approximation, it can try to predict which are the possible levels at which the price can fall and will be ready.

- When the signs of a trend reversal are clear, instead of selling, they will buy. It will buy so low that it will turn this traumatic event for some into a very good profit when the coin rises. Because if the project is valid, it will most likely go back up, it's just a matter of time.

As long as you don't sell, there is no loss, it's just a price difference between the amount you bought and the current market price. **The loss is considered a "loss" when the asset is sold**. Before then, there is talk of unrealized loss.

Rule No. 8: The real loss materializes when you sell.

...

8.2 Losing lucidity

In the trader who loses lucidity, emotionality can unconsciously trigger three types of choices:
1. The "**Fear Of Missing Out**"
2. The "**Panic sell**".
3. The "**blind faith**".

8.2.1 How "Fear Of Missing Out" works

This is what happens in the exact sequence:
1. The **price** of the cryptocurrency **suddenly rises**.
2. In the wake of the increase, a **multitude** of buyers are **attracted** by the possibility of **making profit**, they enter with their purchases, causing a **parabolic increase** in the price.
3. The **price surge ends** when most of the investors, **who were already inside before the pump, sell** to collect their profits (take profit) and the price consequently **drops rapidly**, dragging even the latest buyers into the. Those who are most screwed are obviously the last to buy because, among other things, they also did it at the highest price.

When an event literally causes the price of a coin to explode, even by 100, 200% and even more, the so-called "**Fear Of Missing Out**" creeps in, that is the fear of "missing the train", of losing an opportunity in which it seems that everyone is celebrating and enjoying except those who are left out.

Usually **social media** fuels these events, prices move because they trigger an overdose of **trust**, such as when Elon Musk claimed to have invested a billion and a half dollars in bitcoin with his electric car manufacturing company.

Or even with fake news spread artfully, for the benefit of a few who steal the money of many.

The strong risk is to enter late, to buy when the price is now at its relative maximum and the reversal begins due to the unleashing of the sellers who have satisfied their target and sell by dragging down the price in a steep swoop.

The result for the emotional trader of the **Fear Of Missing Out** is that of a "**buy high, sell low**", the exact opposite of what the trader's bible commands to do. If it does not sell, it will end up with the asset perhaps more than halved or worse with a fistful of flies in hand if the cryptocurrency project is not solid, because it is very unlikely that it will be able to revise the price at the level reached during the pump. And if he sells he will have to resign himself to the loss suffered by the buy high, sell low.

8.2.2 How not to fall victim to the "Fear Of Missing Out"

In order not to be prey to this raptor always ready to strike, here is the strategy of a chess player trader:

1. First, always stick to the main rule of the right mindset: "**do not be ridden by emotions**". The bridle is in your hands, keep your clarity.

2. Be aware that the price of a coin **cannot steadily rise** parabolically forever. A sudden parabolic price increase always corresponds to a correction. The bigger and faster the increase, the stronger will be the correction. Usually follows an accumulation and distribution phase depending on whether the price goes back up or down.
3. **Never buy** when the price is on **relative highs**, it is better to wait for the correction, as long as there is a healthy and valid reason for a new price increase.
4. Make sure that the price increase is not due to a "**Pump and dump**", i.e. a real manipulation of the market by large investors.
1. Basically, one must avoid following the flock of sheep that is being manipulated. A good entry point could be that of **50% of the maximum peak correction.**

8.3 The "Panic sell"

In the panic sell scenario this is the process that takes place in the exact sequence:

1. The **price** of the cryptocurrency **suddenly drops**.
2. In the wake of the downturn many traders sell causing, with their sales, a **vertical drop** in price.
1. The fall in the price **ends** when the price reaches a level that appeals to **buyers who come in and buy at sale prices**. Such purchases will again **raise the market price** of the coin until it finds a **balance** and the accumulation and distribution phase

begins depending on whether the price goes up or down again.

2. Those who get screwed the most are obviously the **last** to have sold because, among other things, they also did it at the lowest price.

It is the **exact opposite of the fear of missing the train** of an undeniable opportunity.

In **falling** markets, so-called **bearish**, when the generalized sale is unleashed, the emotional trader lets himself **be carried away** and sells for **fear** that prices will collapse completely, so as not to find himself with the value of the currency zeroed. Maybe he had done a long study before investing, considering a return on profit within a month. If the purchase was made sensibly, it effectively concedes to the emotionality and fear of losing sight of its time horizon, thus forgetting the strong points of its investment strategy, focusing instead only on the short term.

8.3.1 How not to fall victim to the "Panic sell"

In order not to be prey to this atavistic fear always ready to strike, here is the strategy of a chess player trader:

1. If the purchase was made in a **thoughtful way** and if above all the requirements for which we did it still exist, then there is no reason to sell.
2. It is certainly better to **keep a good investment**, even if it is depreciating **rather than selling everything at a loss**. If the validity of the project still exists, it can be traced back from one moment to the next.

3. Always remember rule no. 6, that the loss is considered such when the asset is sold. Before that, even if the price is lower than the purchase price, it is called an **unrealized loss**. By maintaining the asset, you enable yourself to gain from its future rise and even better performance than before.

   In bearish markets, trend reversal is much more likely than in bullish ones.

8.4 The "blind faith"

Sometimes, especially for inexperienced, that a trader has an attitude of extreme confidence in rising markets.

In the so-called bullish markets, although the price has risen a lot, it is tempting to enter with the belief that the price will continue to rise forever. But it is a big mistake. It is a sort of blind faith that borders on fanaticism and that has nothing to do with the calculation of probabilities and the analysis of the market on which the choices of the entry points should be made.

The harsh law of trading will bring to your senses, after the first substantial losses of money, those who are affected by extreme and blind optimism.

8.5 Summary: "How not to be overcome by emotionality"

1. Emotions are important, the real difference is between **experiencing them and suffering them.**
2. Living them allows us to be free, undergoing them makes us slaves to them, dulls the mind and

makes mistakes not only in life but also in investments.

3. Place purchase and sales orders always concentrated and with the utmost **cool head**.

4. Avoid following the flock and always remember that **"whoever comes later, loses!"** instead the one **who anticipates the market wins**.

5. Information research and **technical analysis** are the determining factors that help us decide when to enter and when to exit.

6. And if we have really missed what we believe was a great opportunity, let's face it and accept the situation. This will allow us to **focus** on investments and not on revenge or revenge.

Live your emotion without being dominated by it, otherwise your choices will lead you to lose money and ruin your investments.

Chapter 9
Understanding when to buy and when to sell

In the world of trading, both the stock and cryptocurrency world, you will often hear this rule mentioned.
Rule No. 9: "Buy deep, sell high".
It is the trader's mantra.
But it's just an idea.
Anyone who tells you it can be done is a cheat.
Of course, even better would be "anticipating the markets", but nobody has the crystal ball that works, otherwise it would be the absolute ruler of the earth.
Determining an entry or an exit point is just a probability calculation, who does his homework better, who gets closer, wins.
There are many techniques, there is no absolute best one because in addition to **technical analysis**, there are many **fundamental analysis** factors to consider.

9.1 Fundamental analysis is made of research, of information drawn from multiple sources. Sources that must be as reliable as possible. Selected sources that everyone gets where and how they can.
There are many variables that can affect the value of an asset and market prices. Sometimes those that come to light are just the tip of the iceberg of what sometimes remains unknown for a long time.
It is like when a couple of people separates and divorces: sometimes the reasons are obvious and are there for all to see, other times an almost insignificant event

happens, which alone could never have the strength to cancel a relationship. Probably the disagreements of a story that for some time now struggled to stand up, but which was unknown to many, sometimes even to those directly concerned, were smouldering under the ashes.

There is hardly just one cause, there are always a series of factors that contribute to determining a specific event, even in the financial markets.

This is the fundamental analysis, the study of what is happening in the market and in the world from a price forecast perspective, including gossip.

Some academics of the financial markets may shudder when they read that I also added the gossip. But how many times have a sentence during an interview or a tweet from an important figure in the world of finance, a head of state, a Federal Reserve executive acted as a trigger in the change in prices?

The stock exchange markets are full of examples.

A great American finance tycoon, a few years ago declared that bitcoin was rat poison, causing many negative influences on those who knew him as the prophet of finance.

But since then bitcoin has grown by more than 2,000%.

Always make your assessments and above all choose reliable information channels, not just those that only tell you what you would like to hear. Also compare yourself with other opinions distant from yours. Comparison is important. But then make your own considerations and make your own choices.

Fundamental analysis is an excellent ally but on its own, however, it is not enough.

A good fundamental analysis cannot be separated from a good technical analysis.

Just as a good technical analysis cannot stand without fundamental analysis.

9.2 Technical analysis, unlike the fundamental one, does not go in search of information. All you need are the charts. The schematic representations of market price trends, which it uses for the "**market action**". Its purpose is to study market **movements** to predict **price trends**.

In the "**market action**" that some improperly call "**price action**", three fundamental factors are taken into consideration:

- **Prices**
- **Volumes**
- **Open interest**

Price is the direct result of all factors.

The **volumes** indicate the amount of exchanges in buying or selling the security under consideration. They indicate the "**sentiment**" of the market in relation to the price trend and identify the mood of investors.

By analysing the **volumes** of a stock it's possible to understand the strength of the trend.

When **volumes grow**, it means that interest in the title increases and this strong trend has a good chance of continuing.

If the **volumes fall**, there is a decline in interest in the stock, if the trend is weak it will not continue in its direction and there could be a trend reversal.

Volumes are very important and it is a big mistake not to

take them into account.

Open interest observes whether **money is entering or leaving the market**. If it **rises** during the phase of an uptrend this is a confirmation and **strength** signal; if open interest **falls** it is a sign of **indecision** and a probable price trend reversal. A **sudden shortage** of open interest for an asset is a signal that the short-term trend **could end** because investors are closing all their positions and that a reversal is to be expected.

...

With these two essential tools, fundamental analysis and technical analysis, you can get anywhere in every financial market, not just cryptocurrency.

People curious by nature usually have an advantage in fundamental analysis, while the more analytical ones have an advantage in technical analysis.

If we want to make a comparison with the academic world, fundamental analysis is a subject of **humanities**, while technical analysis is a **scientific** subject.

The advanced trader will have understood by now that the study and deepening of these two disciplines are a real **investment** for himself, which over time could really make a difference and make him truly rich and free.

I will deal with these two indispensable tools in a **simple** and complete way in my next book. If you are interested, try searching by author to see if they have been published in the meantime.

Chapter 10
Deploy a winning strategy

Now that we covered a lot of different you can finally identify and choose your personal winning strategy.

Yes, **personal**, there is not a single strategy that is suitable for everyone, on the contrary it must be adapted to each individual trader / investor.

In a very simple and schematic way, let's evaluate it together.

Letters correspond to each numbered item, after the "=" sign you will find the recommended procedure to follow. It is up to you to choose the letter that is right for you from among the answers.

1. **Knowledge of trading / investments**
   a) no knowledge = invest in training
   b) medium knowledge = invest the same in training

2. **Experience in trading / investing**
   a) no experience = avoid trading for the moment, devote yourself to active holding with accumulation plans
   b) little experience = trend follower * operation, which considers only the market price trend
   c) good experience = mixed operation
   d) high experience = mixed operations + hedge with derivatives (only if you have extensive knowledge of the subject)

3. Emotional profile

   a) you are anxious person = create the appropriate mindset (see chapter 3) + dedicate yourself to active holding with accumulation plans ¬ + evaluate operations with a wide-ranging time frame

   b) you are calm people = create the right mindset (see chapter 3) + mixed operation

In Chapter 6, with regard to emotionality, we have already given ample space to this fundamental topic that I recommend you re-read.

4. Time available

   a) little time available = avoid trading for the moment, devote yourself to active holding with accumulation plans

   b) average time available = trend follower operation + mixed operation

   c) a lot of time available = trend follower operation + mixed operation

5. Knowledge of the tools

- **Fundamental analysis**

   a) no knowledge = avoid trading for the moment, devote yourself to active holding with accumulation plans

   b) little knowledge = avoid trading for the moment, devote yourself to active holding with accumulation plans

   c) good knowledge = trend follower operations + mixed operations

- **Technical analysis**
  a) no knowledge = avoid trading for the moment, devote yourself to active holding with accumulation plans
  b) little knowledge = trend follower operation
  c) good knowledge = trend follower operations + mixed operations

6. **Capital available**
   a) little capital = active holding with accumulation plans
   b) medium capital = active holding with accumulation plans + trend follower operations + mixed operations
   c) a lot of capital = active holding with accumulation plans + mixed operations + hedges with derivatives (only if you have extensive knowledge of the subject)

10.1 Trend followers

"Trend is your friend" they say in the industry. In practice, the goal is to enter the market where there are signs that a trend is being born, an expansive movement. Whether it is bullish or bearish we do not care because it opens both long and short positions. Look for trends because they are the optimal situations to make a profit.

The main indicator of the trend is the **trendline** of the graph, which by itself unequivocally indicates the direction of the current flow of money. Other useful indicators are the moving averages, the Donchian channels, the ROC and the ADX which, however, must be seen in a context of technical analysis.

Here are the requirements that must be met to start trend following:

1. Recognize the trends
2. Identify the trend and follow it
3. Find the highs and lows of the trends
4. Knowing how to recognize retracements, also called corrections
5. Draw the trendlines

...

Let's now go into the details of each one of them.

10.1.2 Knowledge of trading / investing

"I know I do not know" is the wise and humble inner attitude of those who are preparing to learn a subject unknown to them or that they do not know thoroughly.

Since we are talking about capitals, in this case too, it is a very good idea to invest in one's training.

10.1.3 How to gain trading experience

As each of us well knows, experience is acquired with practice, so here's how to gain experience in the shortest possible time.

- Theory alone is not enough
- Do a lot of simulated trading on demo accounts made available by exchanges platforms or simulate operations by keeping a written record on a notebook or an excel sheet.

- Simulated trading on demo accounts it's useful to become familiar with the platform, but does not protect us from the emotionality of risking your own money. You need real money to educate your emotions, you need to take risks on your own, you need real capital.
- Low capital initially to limit losses.
- Increase the capital hand in hand with the increase in experience
- Try, try, try.

10.1.4 Emotional profile

As we said, emotionality is that thing that makes us react suddenly and abruptly in the face of a situation, if we suffer it, we lose the necessary clarity and fear prevents us from making sensible choices. With regard to emotion, we have already given ample space, in **Chapter 6**, to this fundamental topic that I recommend you re-read.

10.1.5 Time available

Quantifying the time available to devote to operations is important, because it allows you to understand the commitment you are facing. Everyone, based on their time available and their goals, makes their choices regarding their winning strategy. Don't underestimate the "time" variable. The more time you have, the more you can afford a greater presence on the markets, but the greater the stress you are subjected to.

With weekly time frames, a "simple and relaxed" approach is maintained.

With hourly or daily time frames there is a need for greater presence on the markets.

10.1.6 Knowledge of the tools

Fundamental analysis and technical analysis are the essential tools with which you can get anywhere in all financial markets, not just cryptocurrency.

These two disciplines are a real investment in themselves. Over time they really make a difference and make the trader who invests in his training rich and free for real.

10.1.7 Capital available

Simulated trading on demo accounts made available by some exchange platforms are very useful. They are used to familiarize yourself with the platform. But the effect that is generated is like that of Monopoly: buying and selling hotels and companies with fake money involves the player's emotions only in a tiny part. Try to imagine the emotional state of those who are really getting ready to pull the money out of their pockets to buy the electricity company ... Did I make myself clear?

After practicing with demo accounts, it is necessary to raise the level and use real money, just a little at first, but real. Only in this way will you be able to test the effects of your emotions and understand how it is best to act. You need real money to educate your emotions. It takes real capital. Initially low to limit any losses, increasing it hand in hand with the increase in experience.

Rule No. 10: "Strategy indicates direction"

It is up to us to identify our own personal winning strategy.

By looking for your location within the operating profiles listed above, you should have found your location. The one with which you identify best, or at least makes you feel that you are on the right path to have your winning strategy.

Chapter 11
Making a passive income with cryptocurrencies

Sometimes it is really a shame to see your cryptocurrencies in the wallet inactive and useless. There are many ways to create a **passive income** for unused coins. But most of the time it means handing over the private keys of our little treasure into the hands of **strangers**. So, the first thing to do is accurate analysis to get **information** on the **reliability** of these financial services platforms. By putting your coins in the wrong hands there is the risk of losing them all.

By **passive income** we mean that cryptocurrencies are left on deposit on a third-party platform, for a certain period of time, during which an interest is received.

In fact, many of these platforms perform a real banking service, they have even earned the nickname "banks of the future". In effect, the depositor takes the interest and the borrower pays it. All in a very smart and fast way.

But let's see what the selection criteria and the characteristics of a platform that offers this service should be. Here they are in order of importance:

1. Security
2. Offered yield
3. Fees applied and cost of the service
4. Numerous cryptocurrencies accepted
5. Ease of use
6. Number of users
7. Centralized and decentralized platforms

...

I don't want to advertise any platform, but I can tell you which are, point by point, all the characteristics that a top quality one should have. You should make some research if you want to take advantage of this opportunity to obtain passive income from your cryptocurrencies that you do not use.

1) **Security**

This is the first factor, the **determining** one that commands the choice. It is useless to do business with a platform that gives you double the interests of the others if the companies behind it are veterans of other previous bankruptcies or involved in unlawful actions.

- To analyse the platform with regard to security, one must be informed about the companies that own and manage it. Safe ones usually have big, trustworthy names.
- Find out where the office is located. To be safer, the offices must be located in countries where the platforms are regulated, such as in the USA, where the companies that deal with finance are subject to very strict rules.
- Who are the investors. These are usually well-known companies in the industry that have been in the market for a long time.
- What are the guarantees they offer on deposits. The best ones offer complete insurance guarantees: full repayment of the deposited capital in case of hacking or error by the

employees of the company that manages the platform.

2) **Interest offered**: the best ones offer no less than 6% interest on bitcoin, while for the "stable coins" (Usdt, Usdc, etc.) between 8 and 9%, on Ethereum no less than 5%. The returns are paid monthly or weekly.

3) **Applied fees and cost of the service**: they usually do not require fees neither for the deposit, nor for the withdrawal and not even fixed costs to join the platform.

4) **Number of accepted cryptocurrencies**: the wider the offer of accepted coins, the more opportunities there are for users.

5) **Ease of use**: both the proposed system and the user interface must be simple to understand and use, both with a computer and especially with a smartphone.

6) **Number of users**: the best ones have a large amount of users. A few hundred thousand to a few million active users.

7) **Centralized and decentralized platforms**
For this topic it is necessary to make a distinction, the services offered and the platforms are divided into two categories:
- **CeFi** (Centralized Finance)
- **Defi** (Decentralized Finance)

Both have the goal of providing access to financial

markets and financial services for people, but they should not be confused with each other.

In CeFi it is the companies that manage the business and have absolute power over all decisions. In fact, they carry out the operations of a bank: deposits and loans.

In DeFi it is the software grafted onto a blockchain, the "smart contracts" that regulate the functioning of these systems in a completely automated way, without the need for human beings to be present.

11.1 Advantages and disadvantages

Let's see schematically what the mutual advantages/disadvantages between the two categories are.

- **Anonymity**
- In the CeFi, since the platforms are regulated, there is no anonymity.

  KYC (Know Your Customer) recognition protocols and AML (Anti Money Laudering) anti-money laundering protocols are used for registration on the platform.
- In the **Defi** there is anonymity.

  The user does not have to ask for permission to use the platform, there are no entities or states that verify or can censor the DeFi protocol.
- **Flexibility**
- CeFi platforms are flexible, you can deposit different types of currencies, being a company that manages them they have customer support, insurance on deposited funds.

- In DeFi platforms there is not much choice, if you make mistakes you have no one to turn to, no money back to claim.
- **Security**
- In CeFi platforms, the user leaves the private keys to the company and therefore the possession of the funds to the platform.
- In the DeFi platforms, the private keys and possession of the funds are in the hands of the user.
- **Transparency**
- CeFi platforms are managed by companies and the information they filter on their management is only what the companies want to make known.
- On DeFi platforms, each user can read the operations that take place on the blockchain through the dedicated application.
- **Progress and innovation**
- CeFi platforms are preparing to become the banks of the future.
- DeFi platforms are always looking for innovations and improvements to apply to their protocols with the consequent advantage that all fintech will be able to take advantage of these technological innovations.

How do they work?

The use of **CeFi** platforms is **very simple** and this is the great strength that has made these services grow exponentially.

The average user is perfectly able to open an account,

make a KYC registration, understand the use and the returns to be received, the commissions to be paid.

Basically, he **deposits** his cryptocurrencies on the CeFi platform, just as if he were making a deposit in the bank. The company holds its cryptocurrencies and uses them for its own purposes. The customer receives interest on what he has deposited on a daily, weekly, monthly, yearly basis, according to the plan he has chosen.

The other important factor that made these platforms grow dramatically was the fact that, in the event of a **claim**, the platform's insurance **intervenes** to **cover every eventuality**, thus convincing even the most suspicious to leave their coins in the custody of the companies. .

DeFi platforms, on the other hand, **are not very easy to use**: their protocols are substantially different from each other, as are the rules of use.

In an institutional economy, traditionally slow and embalmed, these systems are born and thrive not because of passing fashions but because they are the result of real needs.

What are the reasons?

- In recent years, the banking system has practically zeroed interest rates on money deposited by savers.

   CeFi and DeFi offer potentially much higher returns to their users.

- Currently, more than two billion people do not have access to credit, because they are cut off from the technological gap that exists in many countries of Africa and Asia. But they have access to a **smartphone** and that device can become a bank for them.

In fact, it is expected that within a few years the major users of these services will be them, the ones who are today the most economically marginalized.

Necessity sharpens ingenuity.

...

Rule No. 11: "Rent unused coins"

In light of the arguments seen in this chapter, we have a real example of how to make money work for us.

...

Chapter 12
How to secure accounts and cryptocurrencies

Given its importance, this fundamental topic should have been chapter n. 1.

But if I had put it in the front pages, how would I have made you understand how important it is to secure your bitcoins?

If first you are not aware of the true value of an asset such as bitcoin, how can you appreciate it and give the right weight to its protection?

This was the initial part of the journey we made together.

From the beginning of the book, chapter after chapter, passing through the story of Satoshi and the blockchain, to the invention of money and banks. From the need to create in ourselves the right mindset necessary to face a market populated by bulls and bears, to the ability to overcome the anxiety and panic arising from the fear of losing one's money. From understanding when it's time to buy or sell, to knowing how to recognize and use your personal winning strategy.

I am of the opinion that to truly appreciate something you need to know it.

And experience has taught me that the more you know it, the more you appreciate it.

Something of value must be protected and to do so you need to know how to do it.

Rule No. 12: "Securing accounts and devices"

The secret is to "prevent".

Let's see together what are the best systems to protect bitcoin and cryptocurrencies.

12.1 Securing Your Computer

As a computer scientist, I will make you a list, according to my personal experience, of the commandments to be followed in order to make your computer completely safe.

1. Use a dedicated computer for trading only.

    It means that it should only be used for that. You don't have to do anything else, read your mail, browse websites, or social media. Nothing other than for trading.

    There are computers with Linux operating systems at a very low cost because they don't need a lot of power.

2. The operating system would be preferable if it was not the one with windows. Because they are easy prey for viruses and malware which, once installed, could steal the data to access your wallet or the platforms you use for trading and hackers could steal the cryptocurrencies deposited.

    Statistically, with Mac and Linux operating systems it is much rarer to get hacked. In case you cannot help but use a computer with an operating system with windows it is imperative that you install a reliable and paid anti virus, constantly updated, with which to protect your presence on the web when you connect to your trading platforms or by CeFi / DeFi.

3. It is imperative that you only ever use your computer to connect online.
   Never that of friends, relatives and above all **never** and I **repeat never** an internet point.

4. Always use your secure line if possible with the network cable.

5. If you use a **Wi-Fi** line, make sure it is only yours and that it is protected with the latest security standards provided by your telephone company.
   The Wi-Fi **password** must be very strong to limit the risk of being hacked. And above all never, I stress **never**, connect to public or private Wi-Fi such as those of a **bar** or a **hotel** to trade. **Sniffing** credentials in these places is beyond your imagination.
   When you are in these places, use the data connection of your telephone operator.

12.2 Securing tablets and smartphones

In my experience, I will list the commandments to be followed to make **tablets** and **smartphones** completely safe, some are very similar to the previous ones but, as the Latins used to say, "repetita iuvant" that is, repeating things helps to understand them better.

1. Use a dedicated **tablet** or **smartphone** for trading **only**.
   Here, too, it means that you don't have to do anything else, neither browse websites, nor social media, especially **no texting**: on phones most of

the traps come through the SMS door. Just touch a link on a text message to trigger the hacking of your device. If you are not an actor or famous person for whom they look for your compromising photos for gossip or to blackmail you, then they are looking for identities and cryptocurrencies to steal. Do yourself a favour, use only one for trading. You install your wallet and the apps of the platforms you use on it and use it only for that, thus **minimizing** the risks.

2. To connect online, always use your device only.
   Never enter your **credentials**, nor the **private keys** of your cryptocurrencies on other people's devices, even if you know them and swear you can put your hand on fire for the trust you feel for them. They may have their device **infected** and **not know it**.

3. Always use your data connection to connect to trading platforms.
   If you use a Wi-Fi line, make sure it is only yours and that it is protected with the latest security standards provided by your telephone company.
   The Wi-Fi password must be very strong to limit the risk of being hacked. And above all never, I stress never, connect to public or private Wi-Fi such as those of a bar or a hotel to trade. Sniffing credentials in these places is beyond your imagination. When you are in these places, use the data connection of your telephone operator.

12.3 Secure All Accounts

After securing all the devices you use to do your business it is vitally important to **secure all accounts**. And when I say everyone, I mean everyone including **e-mail, social media**, etc. Here is the list of commandments:

1. **Never** use the **same credentials** on different accounts. This is **imperative**. A **different** user and password must be used for each account.

   Nowadays there are still people who use the same password for all their accounts, it is to shudder. In addition to laziness, their thinking is more or less this: **"anyway I have nothing to hide"**.

   There is nothing more wrong.

   The problem is not that "you have nothing to hide", but the **identity theft** that can result from such wicked behaviour. Identity theft is one of the most rewarding **crimes** on the web. Try talking to people who have suffered it, about the **hell** they had to go through to get out of it. With your identity and in your name they will be able to do anything, the only limit is your imagination. They will be able to buy, sell, defraud, tarnish, open accounts, request funding, stalk, leave your traces in criminal actions, etc., etc. Then go and explain it and bring the evidence to court that it wasn't you ...

2. **Avoid** exchanges and platforms that **do not use the two-factor identification system** like the plague. If you have to put your money in the hands of those people, you start off badly. **Two-**

factor authentication with text messages is the most hackable of all.

It lends itself to the "**sim swap scam**". In practice, the hacker sends you a text message with a link that as soon as it is clicked installs a virus that infects your phone and clones your sim. With the cloned sim, he enters the exchange bypassing the two-factor verification system because the verification SMS reaches him, enters your account on the exchange and takes everything away.

So do yourself a favour: **don't use two-factor verification with texting**.

3. For trading, use large and renowned platforms, **regulated** and recognized, which use two-factor access not via text message. They have been on the market for years, have high transaction volumes, which users speak well of, have good customer care, are secured against platform hacking and offer many services.

   If you **do not use** cryptocurrencies, it is preferable to put them off line on your **hardware wallet** than to leave them stationary on the exchange. Or better put them at **passive income** on a CeFi / DeFi platform.

12.4 The choice of the wallet

In my experience, holding your bitcoins on a **hardware wallet** is the safest system. In this case the private keys of the coins are never exposed, which happens with the computer.

When I send a transaction with the hardware wallet, I

sign the transaction inside the wallet and it is he who does the operation for me. If, on the other hand, I **have an online wallet**, I expose my private key to the web with the **risk** that, if my computer has malware or if my connection is intercepted, the private key is copied and used to empty the online wallet.

Therefore it is preferable to use hardware wallets rather than online wallets.

When choosing a hardware wallet, you are spoiled for choice, there are many, almost all of which are reliable.

My preferences are for those who do not have any type of connectivity with the computer, not even USB or even Bluetooth, always to minimize the risks. There is less exposure and safety is maximized.

In case you do not want to opt for a hardware wallet, as a second choice I would opt for a **mobile wallet** rather than an online wallet that I do not have much confidence. There are several, even here the argument applies that the more they are used and long-lived over time, the more users speak well of them and the more reliable they are.

12.5 Manage the security of the private keys and the hardware wallet seed

As I said, I believe that the absolute best solution for storing bitcoins is the hardware wallet.

*We have seen that the **private keys** are those that decree the **property** of bitcoins.*

*The **seed** is a code, a set of 12, 18 or 24 words without an apparent logical sense, which are used to **restore** the wallet in case of malfunction, breakage, or loss of the* *device.*

Here is an example of a seed: "book november eleven crop river twink game small feet mimic star super".

If the private keys must be safe, the seed must be even more so because, in the event of a wallet failure you need it to access the funds and if lost, they would be lost forever. If someone finds the seed and knows what it is for, they can have full access to all the contents of the wallet.

*Surely it should **not** be stored on your **computer**, not even on a hidden folder or even on an encrypted folder. Unless the computer has internet access, it is disconnected from any network and we are more than sure we are the only ones using it.*

*It definitely **doesn't** have to be stored on the **cloud** and storage drive services, and I'll spare you the reasons.*

*In my experience, the best thing to do is to make **multiple hard copies** and **hide them**. Do not write anything else on the paper so that, even if someone finds it, they would not know what all those words are for without any logical thread.*

12.6 "The honey pot"
I reveal to you a powerful bitcoin offline defence strategy.

To deploy it, you need two hardware wallets. There are some on the market that use a "passphrase" as a security system, in practice the wallet in addition to the 24 words of the seed generates a twenty-fifth word.

All funds are deposited on the wallet with the 25-word seed, except 40 or 50 dollars which are placed as bait on *the wallet with 24 words. The one on which the "**passphrase**" was not generated.*

If for any reason a hacker learns of your seed he will be able to enter the wallet with the 50 dollars, he will think that you are a poor man and it will not occur to him that he has to search for a 25th word to enter a second wallet.

...

Valuable assets and assets must be protected.

*The secret is to "**prevent**". And to do this, you need to know how to do it.*

Now you are able to protect yourself.

Chapter 13
I keep the promise I made to you

Now that you have reached the end of the book, I can finally **keep the promise** I made to you at the beginning: I will reveal the secret to being **profitable in the long run**.

This secret is the "magic formula" that summarizes the exact **sequence** of **operations** that the trader must follow to operate in the markets and be profitable in the **long run**.

It is a **checklist** that must be performed with the exact sequence in which I propose it.

Trading is a complex operation and sometimes even **skipping a single step** can prove **fatal** to its success.

Even after years, when I trade, I keep the checklist **always near to me** and I make sure to tick the items executed one by one until the end. Over time, I have seen my success rate increase considerably.

The items on the list were handed down to me by one of my mentors: John J. Murphy, the author of the trading bible: "Technical Analysis of Financial Markets" to whom I owe a lot despite not having had the honour of knowing him. person.

These secrets are contained in his books and must be known to look for because they are hidden in his pages.

Here is the **list**, in the exact order, of **what the trader in my opinion must do to operate successfully in the markets and be profitable in the long term**.

Checklist:
1. Knowing how to recognize the trend
2. Identify the trend and follow it
3. Find the highs and lows of the trend
4. Knowing how to recognize price corrections
5. Draw the trendlines
6. Follow the moving averages
7. Learn to recognize reversals
8. Learn to recognize the warning signs
9. Follow or not follow the trend
10. Learn what the confirmation signals are

Carrying out this list carefully point by point, when I trade in the financial markets, I have an indicator that constantly tells me where I am and what I need to do to successfully complete my trades.

Some points we have dealt with here in this book, others for reasons of space and the necessary growth over time of the reader I deal with in my other books soon to be published.

If you are interested in continuing to travel with me, do a search by author to see if they have become available in the meantime.

...

Conclusions

I don't want to let you go like this.
To reward your loyalty, I want to give you two more gifts.

1. **Bonus no. 1**

   I reveal my personal orientation.
   I have already included it in the book, but I will propose it again in case you have not been given the attention it deserves. There he is.
   *"The common trader's approach is to focus on the **profit** of the operation. The right mindset of the successful trader, on the other hand, does the opposite: when you go to open a position, you have to **focus** on **risk mitigation** and **capital protection**. The **gain** thus becomes the **natural consequence** of this attitude and not the main thing"*.

2. **Bonus no. 2**

   I feel I can say that in my long personal experience trading and chess have taught me a lot about strategies and knowing how to manage my emotions.
   These are paths that help to get to know each other better. If you find yourself in trouble you can use my mantra to get out of the difficult situations in life. I assure you that it always works with me:

"Do not insist on looking for the solution, if you find the balance it will be the solution".
And I find balance with **meditation**.

...

I sincerely thank you for following me up to here.
Investing in training is equivalent to increasing the value of yourself and is the best choice you can make. Word of a perennial apprentice.
I leave you with this sentence from Albert Einstein that is so dear to me and with the list of golden rules used in the book: "Any fool can know. The point is to understand".

Golden rules used in the book

1. Not all that glitters is gold
2. The blockchain will revolutionize the world
3. Create the winning mindset
4. Find out which companies you are entrusting with your money
5. Prevention is better than cure
6. When you learn to ride a bike, you know how to do it with all bikes
7. Never be ridden by emotion
8. The real loss materializes when you sell
9. Buy deep, sell high
10. Strategy indicates direction
11. Rent unused coins
12. Secure accounts and devices
13. Giving gifts makes us better

...

I wish you **wealth and freedom**.

If you enjoyed the journey we took together, the best gift you can give me is to leave a review on the platform where you bought the book.
Thank you very much.

Francis Flobert
Evolutpress Publisher

Notes